Morning Heart Flow

Evangelist Cohee-Russell

Published by

Radical Women (DBA)
PO Box 782
Granbury, TX 76048
www.bylisabell.com

ISBN-10: 0-9983308-0-9
ISBN-13: 978-0-9983308-0-8

DEDICATION

Dedicated to my loving daughter Chaqoia Gould, who has always been supportive of the things God ordained for me to do. She inspires me to continue encouraging and pouring out words of wisdom to all young ladies and men. So they know that they matter to God, and to me.

ACKNOWLEDGMENTS

I would like to thank my husband, Harold Russell, who always supports, prays and covers me as I stay up late writing, yet wake up early every day to pray and get my grandson ready for school before I go to work. I could never do this without you by my side.

To my son, Hykeem Alexander, who always expresses how proud he is of me. You assure me you are my number one fan.

To my sisters, Kimberley Cohee-Irby and Loretta Phillips. You always express your love and pride for me. To my brother-in-law, Willie Irby, always in my corner expressing the good you see in the work I do. You are a very positive influence and a great supporter.

To my brother, Ray Cohee. You show your love like none other. I love you dearly my brother.

To my church family, those who support and continuously give words of encouragement. To my Co-pastor. Yolanda Butler, who told me to write the book, because of the post she saw me write everyday on Facebook. Pastor Bishop Donald H. Butler who prayed for me and told me I would write books. You gave me the courage to move forward.

To a host of friends and loved ones, thank you so much for all of your words of encouragement.

Day One

God's Plan

> *"For I know the thoughts that I think toward*
> *you, saith the LORD, thoughts of peace, and*
> *not of evil, to give You an expected end."*
> *(Jeremiah 29:11 KJV)*

Sometimes we are so frazzled from everyday life we can't even put our thoughts together.

But God already knows the thoughts He has toward us. They are plans for good and not disaster, to give us a future and a hope. He holds our future, and it's His expected end, not our own. We can plan things that are not

God's plan for our lives. And then we wonder why that thing didn't come through or work out as we planned it.

We must follow God's plan; His will for our lives. So today, pray and ask God that His will be done in your life, and that He will strengthen you to understand what He has purposed and called you to do.

Let's not fall down on the job. Share a word of love, hope and encouragement today. Share the love of Jesus with somebody. Or better yet, share it with everybody you come in contact with today.

Let's be True Disciples of Christ.

Lord, we ask today that You keep us mindful that our ways are not Your ways and our timing is not Your timing. But we must walk in Your will, Your way, knowing You care for us.

In Jesus' name we pray. Amen.

Day Two

Don't be Fooled

> **"And this I say, lest any man should beguile you with enticing words." "For though I be absent in the flesh, yet am I with you in the spirit, joying and beholding your order, and the stedfastness of your faith in Christ."**
> **(Colossians 2: 4 & 5 KJV)**

We must not be deceived with swift talkers and crafty people who may twist the word of God or try to argue their point to justify their actions. The Lord tells us though He is absent in the flesh, He is with us in spirit. He is rejoicing that we are living as we should and that our faith in Jesus is strong.

So we have to have the word on the inside of us. And that way no one can steer us wrong by telling us half-truths and throwing extra words into a scripture to change the true meaning of the Word of God. We have to know this thing for ourselves.

Keep the word of God in your heart that you do not sin against Him. Be thankful. Give God praise ALL day and watch how things work out for you at the end of the day.

No matter what happens, Praise Him.

Lord, today bless us to have the spirit of discernment, to be able to see with our spiritual eye and not get caught up with what we see in the natural. Help us know that things are not always what they look like. And give us the strength to walk in faith, knowing You are always with us.

In Jesus' name we pray. Amen.

Day Three

Go Tell It

> *"Go ye therefore, and teach all nations,*
> *baptizing them in the name of the Father, and*
> *of the Son, and of the Holy Ghost; teaching*
> *them to observe all things whatsoever I have*
> *commanded you: and, lo, I am with you*
> *always, even unto the end of the world.*
> *Amen."*
> *(Matthew 28: 19 & 20 KJV)*

God is giving us instructions, to go teach and train all nations...all races. In the name of the Father, and of the Son, and of the Holy Ghost. To observe all things He has commanded, Jesus tells us, whom He has charged, to carry the gospel.

And those of us He told to witness, which includes everyone who believes in Him, to fulfill the Great Commission. The word "go" means to put in action the word of God.

We can't just sit in churches praising and being spiritually greedy. We have to get out into the streets and witness, carrying a word of encouragement, a word of hope and telling a dying world that Jesus saves! God tells us He is always with us, and if God is for us, He is more than the world against us.

Lord give us Holy boldness to step out and do Your will Your way, knowing You will guide us and direct us all the way. We pray that You will order our steps that we stay in Your will and not get in our own flesh.

In Jesus' name Amen.

Day Four

Know Him

> *"Therefore my people are gone into captivity,*
> *because they have no knowledge: and their*
> *honorable men are famished, and their*
> *multitude dried up with thirst."*
> *(Isaiah 5:13 KJV)*

God tells us His people will go far away into exile. Those who are great and honored will starve, and common people will die of thirst. We must take the time to get to know God.

When we enter a relationship with someone, we take time to get to know them, find out what they like, and what they don't like. We write sweet little love letters to them, and buy them gifts.

Well it's the same way with God. We need to take time to get to know Him. Study His word and find out what He likes and what He doesn't like. The word tells us. "When a man's ways please the LORD, He makes even his enemies to be at peace with Him." (Proverbs 16:7 KJV) We know when we are in a relationship, if all is well and you're pleasing your mate. Or maybe you're not married, but you have a good friend and he or she is happy with you in a friendship, you take time to spend time.

Oh my God; that was deep right there! We don't want to go into exile far away because we didn't take the time to know our God. Let us be found getting in a place to commune with God, to show our love for Him.

Waiting to hear from Him, asking what would You have me to do today oh Lord.

Day Five

Listen and Learn

> **"A wise man will hear and increase learning, and a man of understanding will attain wise counsel."**
> **(Proverbs 1: 5 KJV)**

We are wise; But we need to take time to listen to the proverbs and become even wiser, hear and increase our learning. And if we have understanding we will receive guidance, and wise counsel.

We have to remain teachable because we are forever learning. Stay open to receive, we must not walk in that "I have arrived" spirit. It ain't over until God says it's over, so keep praying, keep reading the Word of God, keep on believing and keep fasting, until the victory is won. Be blessed and let's have a super day in the Lord!

Lord we ask that You increase our wisdom in you. Help us be open to receive instruction and direction knowing that You have our best interest at heart. Help us grow in You and in Your infinite wisdom, knowing who we are and whose we are, and not believing the lies of the enemy. Our desire is to obtain wisdom and knowledge in you. Help us to hear, really hear what you're saying when You speak to us.

Lord let us stay connected to You forever learning and forever gaining understanding and wisdom. Help us to keep a teachable spirit.

We ask this in Jesus' name. Amen

Day Six

Get Wisdom

> **"In the lips of him that hath understanding wisdom is found: but a rod is for the back of him that is void of understanding."**
> **(Proverbs 10: 13 KJV)**

Wise words come from the lips of people with understanding, but those lacking sense will be beaten with a rod. So we must get understanding. The Word even tells us, "Wisdom is the principal thing; therefore get Wisdom; And with all thy getting, get understanding." (Proverbs 4:7 KJV)

We must walk in wisdom getting a full Understanding.

For if not we will be beaten with a rod. The

rod of life – the life of hard knocks. The word also tells us that he who is wise winneth souls.

We must know how to be effective witnesses in our walk with the Lord, and such knowledge comes only from wisdom.

Lord help us to forever seek understanding, wisdom and discernment, so we are not caught up in the cares of this world. Without understanding of a thing, how can we teach or help anybody else? Our desire is to give hope, love and understanding to a world that is dying without hope. Help us not turn our heads to wise counsel. Don't let us go down the road of hard knocks because of being foolish and not wanting to accept words of wisdom.

In Jesus' name. Amen.

Day Seven

Treasure Knowledge

"Wise men lay up knowledge: but the mouth of the foolish is near destruction." (Proverbs 10:14 KJV)

Wise people treasure knowledge, but the babbling of a fool invites disaster. Let's be wise and accept instruction - listen and be teachable. We don't always have to be seen or heard. Sometimes sitting quietly and taking instructions speaks louder than babbling on and not having a full understanding of what you are saying – just being foolish. If we are always talking, when are we able to get instruction and be taught?

We have to realize we don't know

everything about everything. We must continue to be teachable and open to receive what thus saith the Lord. We cannot win souls without God's instructions, and His word tells us that he who wins souls is wise.

Lord, help us continue to store up knowledge and Your wise instructions. Help us put away foolish ideas, foolish thoughts and anything that is not of You. Help us to walk upright in Your sight so others who are looking on don't fall because of anything that we as Christians say or do. Lord, above all, help us bridle our tongues.

In Jesus' name, Amen.

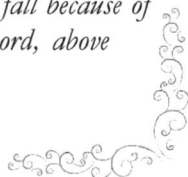

Day Eight

Godly Labor Enhances Our Life

"The labour of the righteous tendeth to life; the fruit of the wicked to sin."
Proverbs 10: 16 (KJV)

The earnings of the godly enhance their lives, but evil people squander their money on sin. No enhancement there.

We have to remember, God gives us instructions in His Word for our earnings. If we earn money God's way, our lives will be enhanced, because we cannot beat God's giving no matter how hard we try. As kingdom builders, we must work according to God's will for our lives to advance the kingdom, knowing we can't beat God's giving no matter how hard we try.

We must understand that God cares about us and our well-being, and if we ask for bread, He will not give us a stone. By following His instructions in giving, we shall receive – pressed down, shaken together and running over, men shall give into our bosom. We will have no lack of anything if we obey the Word of God.

Walk in the spirit of giving to advance the kingdom, and watch God move on our behalf.

Lord, help us be good stewards over our finances. Don't let us be foolish with our earnings. Let us remember to give in our tithes and offerings as instructed by you.
In Jesus' name, Amen.

Day Nine

Guard Your Mouth

> **"In the multitude of words there wanteth not sin; but he that refraineth his lips is wise."**
> **(Proverbs 10:19 KJV)**

Too much talk leads to sin, so we should be sensible sometimes and keep our mouths shut! If you are always talking when do you have time to listen?

Let that marinate for a moment.

A friend once told me that his Dad used to say, "We have two ears and one mouth – we should listen two times more than we talk."

Let's walk in wisdom, listening to instruction and discipline so we don't go astray.

Lord help us not to talk too much so we don't embellish the truth and make up things that sound good but are not about any good. Help us not get caught up in making ourselves look good, for it is not about us, Lord, but all about you. Help us continue to stay focused on who we are and what our mission is here on earth. We don't want to get caught up in getting manly rewards; we strive for the reward of the Lord Most High. In worrying about getting our rewards now, we are saying that what You have for us is not a match for what we are gaining now. Help us know that no good thing shall You withhold from us. So let us grow confident in knowing that what God has for us is for us. No one else can beat God at being God.

In Jesus' name, Amen.

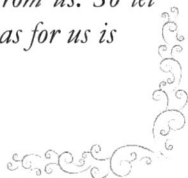

Day Ten

Fountain of Life

> *"The mouth of a righteous man is a well of life; but violence covereth the mouth of the wicked."*
> *(Proverbs 10: 11 KJV)*

The words of the godly are a life-giving fountain, but the words of the wicked conceal violent intentions. These words confirm that God's words speak life to everyone who has an ear to hear. But those who walk in wickedness have underhanded intentions, evil thoughts and evil plans.

We must be careful who and what we listen to. Guard our gates – the things we see and the words we hear. If the sounds and sights do not edify the Lord, then we need to listen or watch something different.

Help us, O Lord, to speak those things that be not as though there were, knowing that You can do anything but fail. We have to realize that nothing is too hard for you, Lord. We must walk in faith believing that we shall have what we decree and believe it belongs to us.

Help us, Lord, to speak into our atmosphere all of the good things that You have promised to us as Your people. Lord don't let us walk in wickedness, selfishness, or negativity. Your promises to Your people are not those of negativity, but of life; and that more abundantly. Keep us positive in you, Lord.

In Jesus' name, Amen.

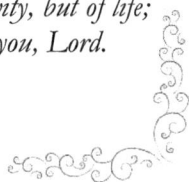

Day Eleven

Remembering the Just

> **"The memory of the just is blessed; but the name of the wicked shall rot."**
> **(Proverbs 10: 7 KJV)**

We have happy memories of the godly, but the name of a wicked person rots away. We want to be sure we live a godly life, so we leave a legacy of good memories.

Walk in love having love one to another that exemplifies Christ in us. No one wants to hear only bad things about their loved ones. Remember we are here but for a while, and we want the family members who are left behind to know our hope in Jesus.

We don't want people to have to be

grasping at straws just to find something decent to say about us after we're gone. And we don't want to put the family on the spot to dig deep or try to fabricate words about who we were, knowing the truth is far from what they say.

Let's live our lives as God instructed. He gave us the blue print for our lives in order to leave a lifelong legacy of love and good memories.

Lord, we pray that You help us not to fail You in this life, knowing if we don't fail You, neither will we fail our families, friends and other loved ones.

These things we ask in Jesus' name, Amen..

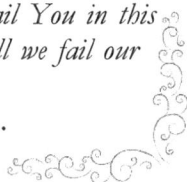

Day Twelve

A Non-Profit Treasure

"Treasures of wickedness profit nothing; but righteousness delivereth from death."
(Proverbs 10: 2 KJV)

Tainted wealth has no lasting value, but right living can save your life. This scripture says it all. It's just that simple.

If our wealth is tainted, then there is no profit in it. God's word tells us the wealth of the wicked is stored up for the righteous. Because the wealth was gotten by ill will, God will allow it to be transferred to the righteous, godly righteous that is. Not those of us who walk in self-righteousness. So let's be sure we pray for true righteousness found in Him.

Lord, help us walk in the righteousness of God. Help us live according to Your will and Your way that we may be saved. Lord, don't let us always try to find the easy way out of things. You blessed us to have a job, and we should be good stewards.

In trying to save money, if we buy items stolen from others, there is no profit for us as Christians. Lord, help us know our every move is a witness to those who live this life looking for hope. Help us be a beacon light to those who don't know Christ as their Lord and Savior.

In Jesus' name, Amen.

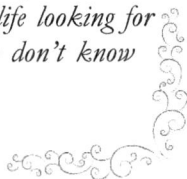

Day Thirteen

Don't be Lazy

> *"He becometh poor that dealeth with a slack hand; but the hand of the diligent maketh rich."*
> *(Proverbs 10:4 KJV)*

According to this Scripture, lazy people will soon be poor and hard workers get rich.

Let's not be slothful in our walk with the Lord, for our blessings hinge on our diligence and our faithfulness to complete the work God gave us to do.

Doors open and fresh new ideas are created to bless us and our families. We must work while it is day, for when night comes no man shall work.

So while the blood still runs warm in our veins, we must be about our Father's business. We need to follow our example, Jesus Christ, who is never too tired to move on our behalf. Morning, noon or night, He is always there to love, to feed us, to keep us in our right minds.

What if God was too tired to move on our behalf? Or what if we called, but He was taking a nap and didn't want to hear our problems at that time. We have to keep pressing forward. We must press toward the mark of the prize of the high calling in Christ Jesus.

Lord, help us and give us added strength even when our physical bodies say no more, but our spiritual body kicks in and says we must press a little bit harder and go a little bit farther.

In Jesus' name, Amen.

Day Fourteen

God's Peace

> *"Peace I leave with you, my peace I give unto you; not as the world giveth, give I unto you. Let not your heart be troubled, neither let it be afraid."*
>
> *(John 14:27 KJV)*

I thank God for this scripture right now in my life. For we need the peace of God that surpasses all understanding.

Nobody can soothe us like the Lord can. And therefore we should not be troubled or afraid, for God has not given us a spirit of fear. God tells us He gives His peace to us. There is no greater peace, and no one on earth can give us peace, joy, and love. God tells us to take comfort; no one can keep us in perfect peace as He can. We must keep our mind stayed on the Lord. So let us meditate on this scripture today as we give God the praise for all He has done, is doing and is going to do on our behalf.

Lord, as we meditate on You today, we ask that You keep our minds, keep our bodies and our soul. Guide us day by day that we not worry about tomorrow; knowing that tomorrow will take care of itself and have its fair share of trouble. But You are in control of all things good and bad.

Help us continue in praise no matter what life looks like. The enemy will always make things seem bigger than what they truly are. Lord, we turn all things over to You, knowing You know just what to do. Keep us in the center of Your will, Lord.

In Jesus' name, Amen.

Day Fifteen

Doing Right Isn't Always Easy

"Blessed are they which are persecuted for righteousness' sake: for theirs is the kingdom of heaven."
(Matthew 5:10 KJV)

God blesses those who are persecuted for doing right, for the Kingdom of Heaven is theirs. We must be found godly righteous and not walking in self-righteousness; that we may be blessed with the Kingdom of Heaven. Even though we may walk through the valley of the shadow of death, we should fear no evil. The Lord is with us. We must realize we will be talked about, cheated on, lied on, and all sorts of horrible things may be unleashed upon us in this world. But the Lord will deliver us from them all.

Lord, as we go through the persecution, and hard times on this earth, give us the strength to trust You. Knowing Your Word is true. David said he was young and now old, but he never saw the righteous forsaken nor his seed begging bread. And Lord, help us to remember there is nothing new under the sun. You are the same yesterday, today and forevermore. The same things You did in Bible days, You are still able to do and are doing in this day. Lord, You are great and worthy to be praised.

In Jesus' name, Amen.

Day Sixteen

Pray One for Another

"Confess your faults one to another, and pray one for another, that ye may be healed. The effectual fervent prayer of a righteous man availeth much."

(James 5:16)

We should confess our sins to one another and pray for each other, so we can be healed. According to this verse in James, the earnest prayers of a righteous person have great power and produce wonderful results. We must stay in a place with God where He hears our prayers and moves on our behalf. We don't have time to get caught up in the cares of this world. We must always be about our Father's business.

Lord, we pray that You create in us a clean heart and renew a right spirit within us. Search us, O Lord, and if there is anything in us that isn't like You, wash us. Cleanse us through and through. For many hurt and need to hear from You, Lord. We need to know we don't have anything hindering our prayers. Help us stay focused on the man in the mirror and not worried about our brothers or sisters who may have a splinter in their eye, when we have a 2 X 4 in our own eye. Keep us with our mind stayed on You so we don't have time to try and figure out anyone else's business.

These things we ask in Jesus' name, Amen..

Day Seventeen

What Good are Riches

> *"Riches profit not in the day of wrath; but righteousness delivereth from death."*
> *(Proverbs 11:4)*

Riches won't help on the day of judgment, but right living can save us from eternal death. We must understand that no amount of money, jewels or precious commodities can get us into heaven. Only by living Holy and being godly righteous will we make it. And the Bible tells us the righteous shall scarcely make it in. So we must continue to pray and ask the Lord to search us, cleanse us from our sins. Anything that is unpleasing in His eyesight, take it away; and in that we have to be willing to let it go. And then shall we be saved from death for all eternity.

Continue searching us, Lord. Even when we don't want to see the ugly inside us. And as You search, show us where we need change, then give us courage and strength to let go of our sin and receive Your healing. Let us desire godliness more than any riches of this world.

In Jesus' name, Amen.

Day Eighteen

Great Value in the Poor

"Blessed are the poor in spirit; for theirs is the kingdom of heaven."
(Matthew 5:3)

God blesses those who are poor and realize their need for Him. Therefore, the Kingdom of heaven is theirs.

So let us not look down on those less fortunate than us, or those who seem to have nothing, because they have the greatest of value according to Jesus. They own the most important thing – Heaven is theirs. We can't have any respect of person, for some have entertained angels and have not known.

We don't want to miss the mark by being

judgmental and critical of people based on how they look, how they smell, and where they live, or what vehicle they drive, or if they even have a vehicle. We must understand, God can turn any situation around. Just when we feel as though we have arrived, God can allow things to happen in our lives and take us to the zero factor in order to humble us. So we must always pray to be humble and godly righteous. Not righteous in our own eyesight, but righteous in the sight of God.

Lord, humble us and fill us with Your righteousness. Where we have self-righteous attitudes, take them from us and replace those thoughts and behaviors with godly beliefs and actions.

In Jesus' name, Amen.

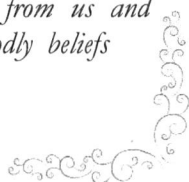

Day Nineteen

Where Our Help Comes From

"I will lift up mine eyes unto the hills, from whence cometh my help? My help cometh from the Lord, which made heaven and earth. (Psalms 121: 1 & 2)

This is where I am today, looking to the hills from where my help comes from. Today is my sister's birthday and extremely hard for me, but I know God will see me through. Love hard on your siblings, children and all family members. It won't make it any easier when they pass on, but you will know you loved that person and enjoyed every moment of life together.

I woke up early this morning, and God gave

me this poem. No, I don't usually write poetry, but He gave this to me in remembrance of my sister.

54 years ago today a beautiful rose bloomed.
This rose has been plucked from my garden,
far too soon.
A rose that stood out from all the rest
A rose that always gave her best.
I loved this rose, she was dear to me,
God took the one and left us three.
I wanted that rose to stay,
at least until today.
But God saw fit to celebrate another way
I love you dear sister
Happy Birthday songs I will sing all day
flowing from my heart…tears.

Lord, remind us to love well those You place in our lives while we yet have the opportunity. For You give none of us a promise of tomorrow.
In Jesus' name, Amen.

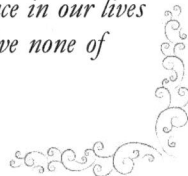

Day Twenty

God Calls us Friend

> *"Henceforth I call you not servants; for the servant knoweth not what his lord doeth: but I have called you friends; for all things that I have heard of my Father I have made known unto you."*
> *(John 15:15)*

Jesus says He no longer calls us slaves, because a master does not confide in slaves. But He calls us friends, because He told us everything the Father told him.

What love! God loves us so much He wants us to get it right; right down here. There is no hidden agenda or secret password, He told us everything. This is an open book test and God shared all of the answers with us because He calls us friend.

Lord, help us so we do not fail You – that we receive the gift, the answers to the test of this life, so we may dwell with You forever.

Help us understand there is no greater love than the love You have for Your people. A love so great You would give Your only begotten son to die for our sins. He who knew no sin took on the sins of the world. That's love.

Lord, we realize there is no greater love than the love You show us daily. And we will forever give You praise, glory and honor, for You alone are truly worthy to be praised,

In Jesus' name, Amen.

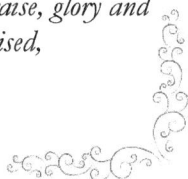

Day Twenty-One

Running Into Your Purpose

"Go ye therefore, and teach all nations,
baptizing them in the name of the Father, and
of the Son, and of the Holy Ghost; teaching
them to observe all things whatsoever I have
commanded you. And, lo, I am with you
always, even unto the end of the world.
Amen."
(Matthew 28: 19 & 20)

God gave us instructions to go, teach, train and equip all nations... all races. In the name of the Father, of the son and of the Holy Ghost. To observe all things He has commanded.

He tells us clearly whom He charged to carry the gospel and those of us He told to witness, which is everyone, in order to fulfill the great commission.

The word GO means to put action to the Word of God. We can't just sit in churches praising and being spiritually greedy. We have to get out into the streets and witness, carry a word of encouragement, a word of hope, telling a dying world that Jesus saves! He tells us He is always with us, and if God is for us, He is more than the world against us.

He came that we might live, and gave so we might be set free, exchanged His life for ours. There is no greater love. So today, if you don't already know what He plans for you this year, ask God. And then take off running into your purpose.

It's a new season, it's a new day, God's fresh anointing has come your way!

Now is the acceptable time, not another second, not another minute. Not an hour or another day, but right NOW! So Lord, give us the strength needed to make it happen.

In Jesus' name, Amen.

Day Twenty-Two

All Things Work Together

**"And we know that all things work together
for good to them that love God, to them who
are the called according to his purpose."
(Romans 8:28 KJV)**

This scripture says it ALL, simply stating ALL things. Everything works together for good to us that love God. We first must love God and not the things of this world. And then we have to be called according to His purpose. We can't get it twisted and state we are called according to His purpose and do any and everything we think we want to do. If our activities are not of God, pursuing everything kills our witness.

We should have the word of God in our heart so we don't sin against God This coming year is a new season, and old things are passed away. Our Greater is coming, and for some it is already here. Let's get on board and get this year started right.

As my Co-Pastor says, "I'm off and running in my 5th season. And I'm Singing – I'm not the same. I have been changed."

Think on these things today. All past hurts are just that – things of the past. But they were needed to push us into our destiny. My Bishop preached on that one Sunday. Take a look at your long gone hurts and see if they didn't push you further along into the direction you needed to go.

Help us, Lord, to see now our past – even the most painful parts – worked to move us where You planned. Give us the courage to look at our hurts with an open heart to see what You had in mind the whole time and then rejoice in what You did through the pain.

In Jesus' name, Amen.

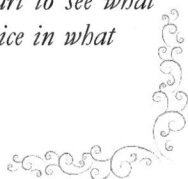

Day Twenty-Three

God's Deliverance

"Many are the afflictions of the righteous: but the Lord delivereth him out of them all."
(Psalm 34:19)

Although we face trouble, trials, and tribulations on every hand, if we put our trust in God – turn everything in our lives over to Him – He will rescue us from ALL of our afflictions each time. We don't have to worry about how to fix the problems. Just turn it over to Jesus, and He'll work it out. Oh yes He will.

Let's not operate as though we are in control—trying to make things happen for ourselves. We must pray and trust God to work all things out on our behalf.

We must take our burdens, our sickness, our financial struggles, whatever our problems are to the Lord and leave them there. Casting our cares on God, knowing He cares for us, and He will take care of us. And in knowing that, we are able to progress forward into our next.

Pray and leave it there. The past is the past and nothing can be done about that, but know who holds the future and celebrate the future. We are truly moving into a New Season.

Walk into or Run into your next season.

Lord, we know You are doing something new. You are always at work around us. Help us put all of our trouble, trials and tribulations in Your hands — and leave them there. You know exactly what to do with each thing that consumes our minds with worry.

As we release all of that to You, give us courage for moving to our new season. Let this next year be the most amazing of our lives, starting today.

In Jesus' name, Amen.

Day Twenty-Four

Don't get Caught Up

> *"Thou therefore endure hardness, as a good soldier of Jesus Christ. No man that warreth entangleth himself with the affairs of this life; that he may please him who hath chosen him to be a soldier."*
>
> *(2 Timothy 2: 3 & 4)*

This passsage breaks down like this – endure suffering along with Jesus, as a good soldier of Christ. Soldiers don't get tied up in the affairs of civilian life, for then they cannot please the officer who enlisted them.

We cannot get caught up or entangled with the cares and drama of this world. We keep our minds stayed on Jesus, who is the author and finisher of our faith. We can't get caught up in vain objects such as clothes, money, fancy cars and big fancy houses. We have a work to do as unto the Lord. We are soldiers, going into the hedges and highways spreading the good news of Jesus Christ.

Strive to please the Lord first. People's words and actions cannot detour us from our mission. We must remember to keep the Main Thang, the Main Thang. Keep your eye on the prize. Remember, this "right here, right now" is not what it's all about. Let that marinate for a minute...hummm. We have to stay on the wall like Nehemiah continuing to work as unto the Lord. Let's move on to our Greater.

Help us, Lord, to keep our mind on You and the work prepared for us. Let us be like Nehemiah, working to please You above anyone and always staying alert at the same time. Move us on to our greater.

In Jesus' name, Amen.

Day Twenty-Five

Count it all Joy

*"My brethren, count it all joy when ye fall
into divers temptations; Knowing this, that
the trying of your faith worketh patience. But
let patience have her perfect work, that ye
may be perfect and entire, wanting nothing."*
(James 1: 2-4)

When troubles come our way, let us count it all joy. Knowing the trying of our faith is making and molding us. Helping us build our patience and faith in God, that we may endure hardship with an attitude of gratitude – going through and growing through.

When our endurance training is complete, we will be fully developed and lacking nothing.

Knowing without doubt, nothing is impossible for God.

And we will know how to wait on the Lord and not move before Him. Not just praying and saying, "I prayed about it." But praying and saying, "I waited on my answer from the Lord as well." Having the patience to wait for God to order our steps and not just taking off in any direction.

Lord, You have already ordered our steps. Help us wait and listen for the order You ordained, especially when hard times come, and we want to call those troubles anything but joy. Give us clear understanding of what You want to teach us during those times.

We believe — nothing is impossible for You.
In Jesus' name, Amen.

Day Twenty-Six

Ask in Faith

> *"If any of you lack wisdom, let him ask of God, that giveth to all men liberally, and upbraideth not; and it shall be given him. But let him ask in faith, nothing wavering. For he that wavereth is like a wave of the sea driven with the wind and tossed."*
>
> *(James 1:5-6)*

James tells us, ask our Father for wisdom because He will give to all men generously. He will not rebuke us for asking.

But we must not waver in our faith, trusting God alone. For if we waver we are unsettled, and we have divided loyalties. Then, we are easily tossed like the waves on the sea, being blown and tossed by the winds.

We have to stand firm and have blessed assurance, not easily shaken or broken. We have to know that no good thing will He (our Father) keep from us.

Wisdom is a good thing. Having wisdom is so important that the Bible mentions this precious gift 222 times. Proverbs 4:7 says, "Wisdom is the principal thing; therefore get wisdom; and with all thy getting, get understanding."

Today, I thank God for another year. I have learned, and I am still learning the wisdom walk with God. We have to operate in wisdom.

Lord help us not to waver in anything that we ask. We do not want to be tossed like the sea, driven with the wind. Continue pouring Your words, Your wisdom and Your will into Your people.

In Jesus' name, Amen.

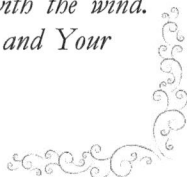

Day Twenty-Seven

We Must Study

"Study to shew thyself approved unto God, a workman that needeth not to be ashamed, rightly dividing the word of truth."
(2 Timothy 2:15)

Work hard so you can present yourself to God and receive His approval. Be a good worker, one who does not need to be ashamed and who correctly explains the word of truth.

We have to get in the Word of God so the Word of God gets in us.

Get the full understanding of what God is saying in His Word. Only then, can we correctly explain the word of truth. We don't want to twist "thus said the Lord."

But we need to know the Bible for ourselves so no one else can tell us anything, and we get fooled, hoodwinked, bamboozled, or led astray by the enemy.

Let's get in the Word and let the Word work in us. It's not going to come by just reading the Bible either. No, we have got to STUDY for the great TEST. We must take the test and pass in order to receive God's best – for the best is yet to come.

Lord don't let us give up during the test. Help us know we have the master note in our notebook and this is an open book test. You allow us to use the book, our notes, and we have the help line to call a friend and get the answer.

In the end, we win

In Jesus' name, Amen.

Day Twenty-Eight

Complaining Displeases God

**"And when the people complained, it
displeased the Lord: and the Lord heard it;
and his anger was kindled; and the fire of the
Lord burnt among them, and consumed them
that were in the uttermost parts of the camp."
(Numbers 11:1)**

We must realize, whatever trouble or trials
we face, we have to go through them with the
right attitude. We do not want to arouse or
kindle the anger of God by complaining,
murmuring and grumbling.

When we do that we are saying we don't
trust God to bring us through or get us out of
the situation.

How can we say we have faith God will bring us out, but turn around and say, "I'm just going through woe is me."

The devil is a liar. The joy of the Lord is our strength. No weapon formed against us shall prosper. This too – whatever your "this too" looks like – shall pass. So we must praise Him in the middle of our through time.

Don't despise the trials – embrace them, and keep pushing in Jesus' name.

Lord, we thank You for every trial and every hardship. For we know they push us to our destiny. The thing You have for us to do on this earth hinges on us passing the tests and trials thrown our way. So strengthen us, Lord, to trust You and believe Your Word is true that You will never leave us nor forsake us. Our blessing, our destiny, waits on the other side of "through." When our fleshly body wants to give up, Lord, keep us spiritually so we press to be blessed.

In Jesus' name, Amen.

Day Twenty-Nine

Pray, Pray, Pray

> *"Watch ye therefore, and pray always, that ye may be accounted worthy to escape all these things that shall come to pass, and to stand before the Son of man."*
> *(Luke 21: 36)*

Keep alert at all times, and pray that you might be strong enough to escape these coming horrors and stand before the Son of Man.

We are supposed to be watchful always. And pray always – pray without ceasing.

I am a living witness that prayer works! It really does change things. And I thank God that when I pray, God hears my prayers and things change. It's not by any goodness of my own. I just have God's favor.

If you haven't developed a prayer life, it's time to get started. Pray when you get up in the mornings. Pray when you get in your cars heading to work, or wherever you're going.

Pray for your children, your spouses, your siblings. Pray about your finances, your jobs or better jobs.

Pray. Pray. Pray! Pray without ceasing. Men ought to always pray. If you don't get much else done today – PRAY! The word tells us to pray that we may be counted worthy to escape all the horrors that are to come.

PRAY.

Lord, if we do nothing else today, help us stay in a constant state of talking and listening to You.

Teach us to pray.

In Jesus' name, Amen.

Day Thirty

Be Slow to Speak

"The heart of the righteous studieth to answer; but the mouth of the wicked poureth out evil things."
(Proverbs 15: 28)

The heart of the godly thinks carefully before speaking; the mouth of the wicked overflows with evil words.

We should study what is about to come out of our mouths, especially if we are in a heated situation. Words hurt and can't be taken back. They cut deep wounds, and sometimes we don't even realize what they did to the person we just said them to.

Sometimes, before you have a

confrontational conversation, write down on paper what you plan to say. Read it to yourself, as if someone else were saying the words to you. See how the conversation makes you feel. If it hurts you or doesn't make any sense to you, then...

Need I say more? Remember, our tongue is a deadly weapon especially in our relationships. Women, men – before you say anything, think on it very hard.

My husband told me once, "Hurt people, hurt people." In other words, people who walk in a spirit of offense or walk in hurt spew out hurtful words or do hurtful things that hurt other people.

Lord, let this marinate in our spirits today. Help us intentionally not hurt others, even in our own pain. In Jesus' name, Amen.

Day Thirty-One

We Must be Godly Righteous

"The Lord is far from the wicked; but he heareth the prayer of the righteous. (Proverbs 15:29)

Let's walk upright before God.

The Bible states Job was an upright man, meaning a righteous man. We don't want to walk in self-righteousness, or in what we think is right. No, we need to be godly righteous.

If you don't know what it means to be godly righteous, pray and ask God to help you understand godly righteousness. Become right in His eyesight.

Then watch how things change for you. The way you look at people, speak to people, treat people, accept people right where they are and love them anyway. All of those things will change for you.

Think on these things today.

God,, we want You to hear our prayers, and we want to be in Your presence in the spirit. We don't want to walk in wickedness. Make us the godly people You desire.

In Jesus' name, Amen.

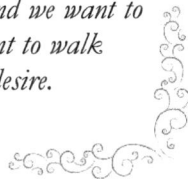

ABOUT THE AUTHOR

Evangelist Clara Russell is the CEO/Founder of Women Walking in Wisdom Ministries. She is a Certified Transformational Life Coach, an Exhorter, Psalmist and Worshiper, committed to reach, teach, encourage, inspire, motivate and empower young women and families to walk in the knowledge and wisdom of God, by applying the word of God to their everyday lives.

A wife, mother and spiritual mother of many children, she loves to motivate and encourage young people, especially women who need to recognize who they are in Christ Jesus. She also enjoys spending time with the seniors, and listening to what they have to say, and catering to their needs.

For more information, visit:
www.wwiwministries.org
www.facebook.com/WomenWalkingInWisdom/